ROTSOME & REPULSANT WORDS

Roald Dahl was a spy, ace fighter-pilot, chocolate historian and medical inventor. He was also the author of *Charlie and the Chocolate Factory*, *Matilda*, *The BFG* and many more brilliant stories. He remains the World's No.1 storyteller.

Yours sincerely
The Roald Dahl Story Company Limited

OXFORD
UNIVERSITY PRESS

Great Clarendon Street, Oxford OX2 6DP

Oxford University Press is a department of the University of Oxford. It furthers the University's objective of excellence in research, scholarship, and education by publishing worldwide. Oxford is a registered trade mark of Oxford University Press in the UK and in certain other countries

Original text by Roald Dahl © 2019 Roald Dahl Story Company Limited
Compilation and additional material © 2019 Oxford University Press
Illustrations copyright © Quentin Blake 2019
Chief editor and lexicographer Dr Susan Rennie

The moral rights of the author have been asserted

Database right Oxford University Press (maker)

First published 2019

British Library Cataloguing in Publication Data

Data available

ISBN 978-0-19-277197-1

1 3 5 7 9 10 8 6 4 2

Printed in Great Britain

Paper used in the production of this book is a natural, recyclable product made from wood grown in sustainable forests. The manufacturing process conforms to the environmental regulations of the country of origin.

Illustration credits: Reproduced by permission of Penguin Books Ltd.

t = top b = bottom r = right

Front cover: *The Twits* (Jonathan Cape, 1980) Illustrations copyright © Quentin Blake 1980. *George's Marvellous Medicine* (Jonathan Cape, 1981) Illustrations copyright © Quentin Blake 1981. **Inside pages:** *The BFG* (Jonathan Cape, 1982). Illustrations copyright © Quentin Blake 1982. 1; 3; 9; 10-11; 24-25; 26-27; 30-31; 37; 38; 39; 44; 57. *Charlie and the Chocolate Factory* (Puffin, 1973) Illustrations copyright © Quentin Blake 1995. 12; 22; 23; 32-33; 39; 58; 59; 60; 63. *The Twits* (Jonathan Cape, 1980) Illustrations copyright © Quentin Blake 1980. 5; 28; 36; 42; 43; 48; 50-51. *Matilda* (Jonathan Cape, 1988) Illustrations copyright © Quentin Blake 1988. 13; 14; 15 b r; 16; 17; 34-35; 61; 64. *George's Marvellous Medicine* (Jonathan Cape, 1981) Illustrations copyright © Quentin Blake 1981. 4; 15 t r; 18; 19; 52. *The Witches* (Jonathan Cape, 1983) Illustrations copyright © Quentin Blake 1983. 6; 40; 41; 46; 47; 54; 55. *The Enormous Crocodile* (Jonathan Cape, 1978) Illustrations © Quentin Blake 1978. 7; 53. *Esio Trot* (Jonathan Cape, 1990) Illustrations © Quentin Blake 1990. 20-21.

We have tried to contact all copyright holders, but should there be any errors or omissions, we will be pleased to rectify them at the earliest opportunity.

ROALD DAHL'S
ROTSOME &
REPULSANT
WORDS

Original text by
Roald Dahl

Illustrated by
Quentin Blake

Compiled by
Susan Rennie

OXFORD
UNIVERSITY PRESS

CONTENTS

Introduction

Have you noticed how some grown-ups use the same rude words and phrases *over and over again*? Most grown-ups think there are only a few rude words in the world. But in fact there are **squillions** of them—and the best ones are the ones you make up yourself, as only you know what they *really mean*.

We have gathered together the most outrageously **rotsome** and **repulsant** words from Roald Dahl's stories—and in case you run out of those, we will also show you how to create your own. (Note that you won't find the REALLY rude words here that Farmer Bunce shouts at Mr Fox. Those are SO RUDE that many grown-ups have never heard of them either.)

No one is suggesting that you run about cursing like a giant all day long. How very boring that would be!

For just like Magic Fingers, rude words have a strange power that comes from saving them up to use *at just the right time*.

Roald Dahl made up more **redunculously** rude words than any other writer. So learn from the best. The grown-ups will never know.

Susan Rennie

A rude word is one that grown-ups do not like you to use, even if they use it themselves

—Oxford Roald Dahl Dictionary

HOW TO Curse LIKE A giant

Giant curses sound a bit like grown-up curses, but no one knows exactly what they mean, so it is perfectly fine to print them in a book, or to say them out loud.

bopmuggered *adjective*

If a giant says he is *bopmuggered*, he is in a very sticky situation and is NOT HAPPY about it. It is very rude to say you are *bopmuggered,* which is why giants like to say it.

'I is bopmuggered!' screeched the Butcher Boy.—THE BFG

Other **gigantuously** rude words which mean the same thing are:

crodsquinkled *adjective*
fluckgungled *adjective*
flushbunkled *adjective*
goosegruggled *adjective*
gunzleswiped *adjective*
slopgroggled *adjective*
splitzwiggled *adjective*
swogswalloped *adjective*

Well, I'll be fluckgungled!!

Now we're goosegruggled!

Giants are also experts at HURLING INSULTS at each other. Here are some of their best ones.

Prunty little pogswizzler!

Squinky little squiddler!

Piffling little swishfiggler!

grobsquiffler *noun*
If you call someone a *grobsquiffler*, you are saying
they are silly and not important.

'Now then, you little

grobsquiffler!'

boomed the Fleshlumpeater.
—THE BFG

pogswizzler *noun*
A *pogswizzler* is a very rude name that the other
giants call the BFG.

squinky squiddler *noun*
Something *squinky* is small and unimportant.
It is very rude to call someone *squinky*, and
even more rude to call them a **squinky squiddler**.

swishfiggler *noun*
A *swishfiggler* is a very rude name that giants
sometimes call each other.

troggy *adjective* **troggier, troggiest**
Something *troggy* is vile and horrible. *Troggy* is a
very strong word, so only *troggy* giants use it as
an insult.

The giants picked up rocks and hurled them after him.
He managed to dodge them. 'Ruddy little runt!' they
shouted. 'Troggy little twit!'—THE BFG

MAKE UP YOUR OWN
gigantuous CURSE WORD

Mix the start of one giant rude word with the end of a different one to make a rude word that *no **human bean** has ever heard before.*

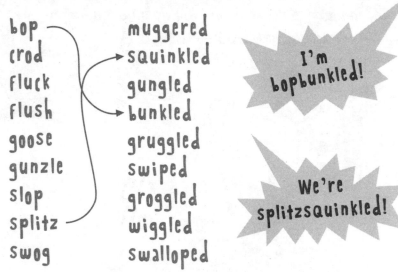

bop	muggered
crod	squinkled
fluck	gungled
flush	bunkled
goose	gruggled
gunzle	swiped
slop	groggled
splitz	wiggled
swog	swalloped

I'm bopbunkled!

We're splitzsquinkled!

Rotsome words are very flexible (a bit like **Vermicious Knids**). You can bend them into other types of word that sound *even rotsomer*. You can make any of these **gigantuous** curse words into INSULTS or EXPLETIVES.

For example, if a beastly grown-up calls you:

You squinky little crodsquinkle!

You could reply:

You ghastly grown-up gunzleswipe!

Or a giant who is RAGING (because you have fed him a snozzcumber), might say:

Swogswallopers!

or even **Bopmuggerly swogswallopers!**

!!ROTSOME TIP!!
An EXPLETIVE is what you say out loud when you are REALLY annoyed about something. It is not the same as an INSULT, as you are not saying it to anyone in particular. See Explosive Expletives on page 56.

HOW TO INSULT LIKE A Trunchbull

'You ignorant little slug!' the Trunchbull bellowed. 'You witless weed! You empty-headed hamster! You stupid glob of glue!'
—MATILDA

Miss Trunchbull likes nothing better than to insult her pupils, and she uses some clever techniques to make her insults even more effective.

You ignorant little slug!

A *slug* is a small, soft animal that looks like
a snail but has no shell.

You festering gumboil!

A *gumboil* is a painful swelling caused by an infected
tooth. (It is important NOT to confuse it with a *gumball*,
which is a hard ball of chewing gum—as only one of
them is nice to chew.)

You fleabitten fungus!

A *fungus* is a plant without leaves or flowers that grows
best in dark, moist places. Mushrooms and toadstools
are types of fungus.

This poisonous pustule!

A *pustule* is an infected blister or pimple.

'This clot,' boomed the Headmistress . . .
'this black-head, this foul carbuncle, this
poisonous pustule that you see before you is
none other than a disgusting criminal!'
—MATILDA

15

Here are some other things that make **slimacious** insults:

SNOZZCUMBER

BLANCMANGE

MUCUS

SEMOLINA GLOOP

FROGSPAWN

!!ROTSOME TIP!!
Note that *mucus* is a noun, but *mucous* is an adjective, so you would say: *You mucous mound of mucus!*

Trunchbull Technique no.2: Use alliteration

Alliteration is when you use the same **Lovely Letter Lots** of times.

You clotted carbuncle!

You stupid glob of glue! You witless weed!

You empty-headed hamster!

16

carbuncle *noun*

A *carbuncle* is a large swollen boil on your skin, so to call someone a *carbuncle* is not nice at all, which is why Miss Trunchbull likes to say it—even though she is the most Beastly Carbuncle of them all.

Trunchbull Technique no.3: BELLOW!

There is no point in coming up with a **rotsomely** good insult if no one can hear it. Think of what you are going to say. Then take a **gigantuous** breath, and . . . **BELLOW!!**

Instant Insult-Maker

To make up your own Trunchbull-isms, try this **Instant Insult-Maker Formula**. It is even more effective if you use alliteration—and always remember to BELLOW!

You ⟨ *adjective* ⟩ ⟨ *noun* ⟩ of ⟨ *noun* ⟩

Examples:

You **big blob** of **blancmange!**

You **glutinous glob** of **glue!**

HOW TO BE AS Grumpy AS A Grandma

Some grandmas, like Grandma Georgina and George's grandma, get very grumpy, and it makes them feel better to curse and say rude words to show how cross they are. (In fact, cursing usually makes *any* grown-up feel better, which is why so many of them do it.)

Grandmothers are especially good at insults, perhaps because they have had a long time to practise. George's grandma calls him:

a disgusting little worm!
a nasty little maggot!

Charlie's Grandma Georgina doesn't trust Willy Wonka and often calls him rude names, such as **You miserable old mackerel!** It is very rude to call someone a *mackerel*, which is why she likes saying it so much.

'You miserable old mackerel!' *said Grandma Georgina, sailing past him. 'Just when we start having a bit of fun, you want to stop it!'*
—CHARLIE AND THE GREAT GLASS ELEVATOR

* * ROTSOME FACT * *
The word *insult* means literally to 'jump on' someone. It is related to *salmon*, which means a 'leaping fish'—so it is doubly insulting to call someone a *salmon*!

HOW TO BE rude backwards
(the ESIO TROT way)

If you've read *Esio Trot*, you'll know that **Saying Things Backwards** is essential for communicating with tortoises. For example:

Tahw a ylevol ecuttel fael!

=

What a lovely lettuce leaf!

But saying things backwards is also a **redunculously** good way of saying **EDUR SDROW** without grown-ups noticing (unless they can speak Tortoise of course).

This technique works best in small doses (like **Wonka-Vite**). If you use it too often, grown-ups might crack the code, and then you will be in **GIB ELBUORT**.

mub → Example: Miss Trunchbull has a **gib mub**!

ylgu → Example: Aunt Sponge is **ylurt ylgu**!

yllis → Example: The President is a **yrev yllis nam**!

!! ROTSOME TIP !!
Note that you reverse the order of letters in each word, but not the order of words in a sentence—otherwise tortoises will be BIFFSQUIGGLED!

HOW TO SPEAK MIDEOUS Martian
(THE WILLY WONKA WAY)

When Willy Wonka pretends to be a Martian, he makes up a string of **redunculous** words to shout at the President of the United States (who is being very silly and thoroughly deserves it). He is therefore able to be very rude without the President (or his Chief Interpreter) having a clue what he is saying.

You can try this, too, either to the President or to another grown-up who is being equally silly. When they don't understand you, just tell them you are speaking Martian.

Mideous Martian technique no. 1: YUBEE LUNI!

This a very useful Martian phrase for telling a President or other grown-up that they are being silly.

Charlie's eyes were riveted on Mr Wonka. … He put so much force into his voice that the effort lifted him right up on to the tips of his toes.

'BUNGO BUNI
DAFU DUNI
YUBEE LUNI!'

—CHARLIE AND THE GREAT GLASS ELEVATOR

You can make your own variations on this, by using a different Martian word after **YUBEE**. For example:

YUBEE SILI BILEE

YUBEE KRAZI PREZI DENTEE

Mideous Martian technique no. 2: ZOONK!

ZOONK is probably a very rude word in Martian, although no one knows exactly what it means. It is best to say it many times over, as fast and as loud as possible.

The next time Mr Wonka spoke, the words came out so fast and sharp and loud they were like bullets from a machine-gun. **'ZOONK-ZOONK-ZOONK-ZOONK-ZOONK!'** *he barked.*—CHARLIE AND THE GREAT GLASS ELEVATOR

An interesting variation is to say **ZOONK** at the end of every phrase, in a threatening manner.

Mr Wonka paused dramatically for a few seconds. Then he took an enormous deep breath and in a wild and fearsome voice, he yelled out:

'KITIMBIBI ZOONK!

FUMBOLEEZI ZOONK!

GUGUMIZA ZOONK!

FUMIKAKA ZOONK!

ANAPOLALA ZOONK

ZOONK ZOONK!'

—CHARLIE AND THE GREAT GLASS ELEVATOR

HOW TO BE rude IN OTHER LANGUAGES

(SO GROWN-UPS WON'T NOTICE)

For centuries, grown-ups have used **rude** and **rotsome** words from other languages to curse and insult each other, so that people wouldn't know what they *really* meant. You can do this too.

Learning **rotsome** words in other languages in ESPECIALLY useful if your grown-ups have already looked up all the rude words in the *Oxford Roald Dahl Dictionary*. But they won't find these words there, so they will be thoroughly **biffsquiggled** when you use them.

beschwipsduselt *adjective*
(say bee-**shwips**-dooz-elt)
a word said by German giants when
they've had too much to drink

furripanchoso *adjective*
(say furry-pan-**choh**-zoh)
a word said by Spanish giants which has
nothing to do with *furry sizzlepans*

gulliewullied *adjective*
a word said by Scottish giants which has something
to do with being stuck in a bog

The German word for a snozzcumber is

Kotz

26

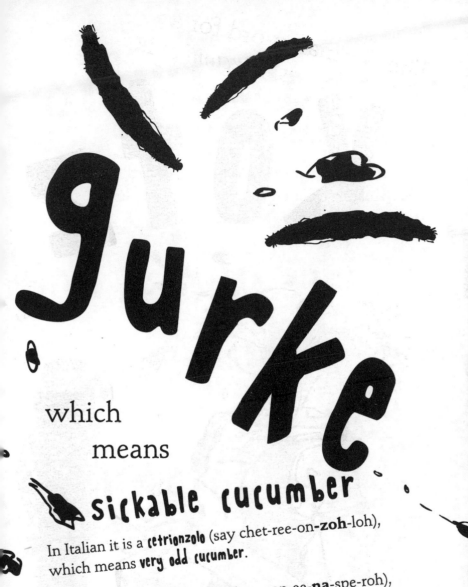

gurke

which

means

sickable cucumber

In Italian it is a **cetrionzolo** (say chet-ree-on-**zoh**-loh), which means **very odd cucumber**.

In Spanish it is a **pepináspero** (say pep-ee-**na**-spe-roh), which means **sour cucumber**.

In Scots it is a **feechcumber**, which translates as **yuck-cumber**.

Troggy TERMS FOR Twits

(AND OTHER BEASTLY BEINGS)

Mr and Mrs Twit are **mideously** mean to each other (and even worse to children and animals). They love to call each other NASTY NAMES, such as

grizzly old grunion!

rotten old turnip!

filthy old

Mrs Twit . . . suddenly called out at the top of her voice,
'Here I come, you grizzly old **grunion**! *You rotten old* **turnip**!
You filthy old **frumpet**!'—THE TWITS

frumpet *noun*

If you call someone a *frumpet,* you mean that they are
old and unattractive. It is very mean to call someone a
frumpet, which is why Mrs Twit enjoys saying it.

ROTSOME FACT
The word *frumpet* may be based on *frump*, which
has a similar meaning and comes from an older
word *frumple* meaning 'wrinkle'.

grunion *noun*

A *grunion* is a very mean or grumpy person. George also
calls his grandmother a **grizzly old grunion**.

Frumpet!

Mrs Twit could have used these other **vegitibbles** to describe her husband, too:

frumpkin *noun*

A *frumpkin* is a vegetable used to make *frumpkin pie*. Unlike the **snozzcumber**, it is good to eat and its name suggests it looks or tastes a bit like a pumpkin.

wurzel *noun*

A *wurzel* is a yellow root vegetable that is fed to farm animals. It is very rude to call someone a **wurzel** (or worse, a **snozzcumber**).

You frumptious old frumpkin!

You wizened old wurzel!

You silly snozzcumber!

Warning!

It is never a good idea to call a

GIANT

a silly

Snozzcumber

unless you have a very good escape plan
(such as hiding inside a *snozzcumber*).

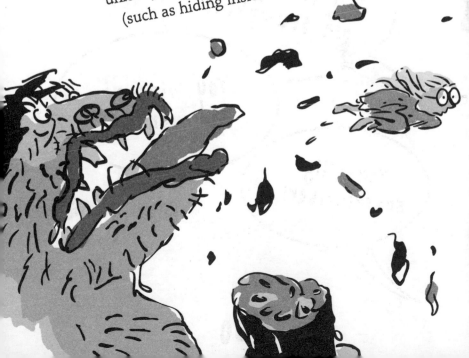

Other words for mean
(or just silly) human beans

grinksludger *noun*

A *grinksludger* is a mean and nasty person, like the *grinksludging* Farmers Boggis, Bunce and Bean.

nincompoop *noun*

A *nincompoop* is a very silly person, for example Augustus Gloop, the *great big greedy nincompoop*.

the great big greedy

rotrasper *noun*

A *rotrasper* is a thoroughly beastly grown-up, like Mrs Clonkers or Miss Trunchbull.

'She locked us in the dark cellar for a day and a night without anything to eat or drink.' 'The rotten old rotrasper!' cried the BFG.—THE BFG

!!ROTSOME TIP!!
Try rolling the R sound at the start of a word like RRRRROTRASPER until you sound like the Grrrrrand High Witch. This will make your curses and insults sound more menacing.

nincompoop

squeakpip *noun*

A *squeakpip* is a very unimportant and silly grown-up.

*'Human beans is thinking they is very clever, but they is not.
They is nearly all of them notmuchers and squeakpips.'*
—THE BFG

squifflerotter *noun*

A *squifflerotter* is a mean and nasty grown-up.

*'Grown-up human beans is not famous for their kindnesses.
They is all squifflerotters and grinksludgers.'*
—THE BFG

vermicious *adjective*

Something *vermicious* is vicious and nasty, just like a Knid.

*'It's worse than that!' cried the
Chief of Police. 'It's a vermicious Knid!
Oh, just look at its vermicious gruesome face!'*
—JAMES AND THE GIANT PEACH

The VERY BAD dreams that the
BFG catches are called

bogthumpers, grobswitchers
and **trogglehumpers.**

These also make good names for mean human beans.

Examples:

Aunt Spiker is a rotten old **grobswitcher!**

Miss Trunchbull is a mean and nasty **bogthumper!**

ROTSOME FACT

It's not just Knids that are vermicious! The word *vermicious* means 'worm-like', which is exactly how George's grandma describes him.

Repulsant WORDS FOR ROTSOME THINGS

Have you ever come across something as *filthsomely foul* as Mr Twit's beard? Or as *oozingly icky* as Farmer Bunce's doughnuts? There are lots of truly revolting things in Roald Dahl's stories, but he never runs out of words to describe them. Take **snozzcumbers**, for example.

'It's disgusterous!' the BFG gurgled. 'It's sickable! It's rotsome! It's maggotwise! Try it yourself, this foulsome snozzcumber!'
—THE BFG

All these words mean 'digusting' or 'repulsive' and perfectly describe a **snozzcumber** or other **rotsome** things.

bogrotting *adjective*

disgusterous *adjective*

filthsome *adjective*

foulsome *adjective*

grizzling *adjective*

grobswitchy *adjective*

icky-poo *adjective*

maggotwise *adjective*

muckfrumping *adjective*

repulsant *adjective*

rotsome *adjective*

sickable *adjective*

ucky-mucky *adjective*

uckyslush *adjective*

'Every human bean is diddly and different. Some is scrumdiddlyumptious and some is uckyslush.'
—THE BFG

!!ROTSOME TIP!!

The word *disgusterous* starts with *disgusting* but has a different ending which makes you think of *dangerous* or *murderous*, as if snozzcumbers taste like deadly poison. To make the word *icky-poo*, Roald Dahl may have started with *icky* and then added *poo* (which is icky too).

Be snozzcumbersome!

You can also make your own words based on **snozzcumber** to describe something **disgusterous**. for example:

That's the most

snozzcumberish,
snozzcumberous,
snozzcumbersome,
snozzcumberumptious

thing I've ever tasted!

YET MORE Rotsome THINGS

grimesludge *noun*

Grimesludge is thick and dirty mud.

'By goggles,' he said, taking the jar out of the suitcase, 'your head is not quite so full of grimesludge after all!'—THE BFG

slubber *noun*

Slubber is a kind of muddy sludge found in boggy places.

slutch *noun*

Slutch is anything that looks or tastes revolting, like a bite of **snozzcumber**.

'That is the most disgusterous taste that is ever clutching my teeth! You must be buggles to be swalloping slutch like that!'—THE BFG

swatchwallop *noun*

Swatchwallop is the most disgusting thing you can imagine eating.

'By goggles!' he cried. 'This stuff is making snozzcumbers taste like swatchwallop!'
—THE BFG

trogfilth *noun*

Trogfilth is disgusting filth which tastes revolting.
Snozzcumbers taste of *trogfilth*.

Roald Dahl once said:

If you have good thoughts they will shine out of your face like sunbeams and you will always look lovely.—THE TWITS

To make this apply to **TWITS**, **WITCHES** or other beastly beings, just use the opposite words:

If you have ~~good~~ **BAD** thoughts they will ~~shine out of~~ **OOZE FROM** your face like ~~sunbeams~~ **SLIME** and you will always look ~~lovely~~ **REPULSANT**.

More than rotsome?

What if something is more rotsome than rotsome? You can use a COMPARATIVE or SUPERLATIVE ending to make a word **rotsomER** or **rotsomEST**.

Example:
That cheese is **rotsomer** *than a snozzcumber.*
Try making up you own comparatives and superlatives for some of the **repulsant** words in this book.

Example: *Farmer Bean is the* **squifflerottenest** *human bean ever.*

REDUNCULOUS
WORDS FOR RATHER

RUDE THINGS

'If everyone is making whizzpoppers, then why not talk about it?'—THE BFG

bottom noun
Your bottom is the part of your body that you sit on. **Vermicious Knids** have pointy bottoms which are not very good for sitting but make good weapons.

'Hello, you great Knid! Tell us, how do you do?
You're a rather strange colour today.
Your bottom is purple and lavender blue.
Should it really be looking that way?
—CHARLIE AND THE GREAT GLASS ELEVATOR

Some grown-ups try to avoid saying the word **bottom**, even though it is a perfectly sensible word. They use all sorts of **redunculous** words instead, which mean the same thing, like *posterior*. They will even say it in French, calling it a *derrière* (which rhymes with *were*).

41

Some other words for 'bottom' you will find in Roald Dahl's stories are:

behind, rear + rump

Mrs Salt . . . was now kneeling right on the edge of the hole with her head down and her enormous behind sticking up in the air like a giant mushroom.
—CHARLIE AND THE CHOCOLATE FACTORY

*I sat. I screamed. I jumped a foot!
Would you believe that I had put
That tender little rump of mine
Upon a giant porcupine!*
—DIRTY BEASTS

Oh, K-nids' K-nickers!

42

knickers *plural noun*

Knickers are underpants for girls or women. The word is a short form of *knickerbockers*, a type of knee-length trousers named after Diedrich *Knickerbocker,* a character in an American story.

As she floated gently down, Mrs Twit's petticoat billowed out like a parachute, showing her long knickers.
—THE TWITS

Note that the phrase **Knids' Knickers** is NOT alliterative, as *Knid* is pronounced with a K at the start (just like the words *knight* and *knock* used to be). To make it more fun AND alliterative, why not pronounce both words with a K?

whizzpopper *noun*

A *whizzpopper* is the noise that comes out of your bottom when you drink too much fizzy **frobscottle**. (It even happens to the Queen.) It is not a rude word (or sound) to giants—just to human beans.

'I has Her Majester's permission!' cried the BFG, and all at once he let fly with a whizzpopper that sounded as though a bomb had exploded in the room.—THE BFG

In giant languages around the world, **whizzpoppers** are called:

flitspoppers (Dutch)

furzelbäume (German)

popotraques (Spanish)

rummlypumps (Scots)

** ROTSOME FACT **

The word *whizzpopper* is ONOMATOPOEIC, which means that it sounds like the thing it describes. Some old words for *whizzpoppers* are squib, poot and crackeret.

Time-twiddling
Curses
FROM LONG LONG AGO

In Giant Country, a *time-twiddler* is someone who lives for a **gigantuously** long time (as all giants do). A time-twiddling word is one that is very old, too, or that was used long ago.

Here are some time-twiddling curses and insults that were said by cross human beans long long ago. Some of them sound just like words you might hear in Giant Country!

bescumber *verb*

To *bescumber* is an old word which means 'to poo upon' someone. If you are VERY BRAVE, you could say to the Grand High Witch:

May bats bescumber you!

But be warned: although it will be great fun, it may well be the last thing you will ever say.

dunderhead *noun*

A *dunderhead* is a very stupid person. Charles Dickens once described a characer as the *dunderheaded king of the noodles*—so you could say that Mr Twit is the **dunderheaded king of Squiggly Spaghetti!** And talking of pasta . . . the word *macaroni* also used to mean a *dunderhead* or very silly grown-up.

∗∗ ROTSOME FACT ∗∗

Charles Dickens was a favourite author of both Roald Dahl and the BFG. The BFG's name for him is *Dahl's Chickens*.

flibbertigibbet *noun*

A *flibbertigibbet* is someone who won't stop chattering. It is an *onomatopoeic* word, which sounds like what it means.

If you say *flibbertigibbet* over and over again, you will start to sound like one!

fopdoodle *noun*

A *fopdoodle* is an old word for a very silly person. If Mr and Mrs Twit had lived hundreds of years ago, they would have been called Mr and Mrs Fopdoodle. Note that this word is not related to **whangdoodle** (a terrifying creature from Loompaland) or to **bunkdoodle** (which means to give you nightmares), although it is possible to say:

That fopdoodle has been

ninnyhammer *noun*

Hundreds of years ago, silly people were called *ninnyhammers*. This would be a splendid insult for Miss Trunchbull to use, because her favourite sport is throwing the hammer (as well as throwing children with pigtails).

numbskull *noun*

A *numbskull* is someone whose head is emptier than a **bundongle**. You could also call them a **cloudbrain**—but be careful not to say this to Cloud-men, or they will get very angry and hurl hailstones down at you.

bunkdoodled by a whangdoodle!

slubberdegullion *noun*

A *slubberdegullion* is someone who is very sloppy and messy, so it is a perfect word for Mr Twit. It comes from an even older word, to *slubber*, meaning 'to smear'.

zoodikers!

This ancient curse word sounds like something Willy Wonka would say to the President.
You could also say **zookers**, **zoonters** or just **zooks**!

Zooks! What a slubberdegullion!

Words that turn UPSIDE-DOWN (slowly)

Twits are not the only things that turn upside down! Did you know that a word can start off as a perfectly nice and polite word, but then change over time to become something **not-so-nice?**

For example . . .

naughty *adjective*

The word *naughty* is related to *nought* and originally meant 'very poor'. It later came to mean 'wicked' and then just 'badly behaved'. So originally, it was poor Charlie Bucket who was *naughty*, not the greedy Augustus Gloop!

silly *adjective*

The word *silly* originally meant 'very good or worthy' and was also used as a surname. In the Middle Ages, being called Mr or Mrs *Silly* was like being called Mr or Mrs *Good* (not Mr or Mrs Twit).

BUT ON THE OTHER HAND...

nice *adjective*

The word *nice* originally meant 'silly or foolish'—not pleasant at all! In other words, long long ago, Mrs Twit would have been a very *nice* person.

Extra-usually
Silly Similes

When you describe something by comparing it to something else, you are using a SIMILE.

'You is only interested in guzzling human beans.' 'And you is dotty as a dogswoggler!' cried the Bloodbottler.—THE BFG

Similes make splendiferous insults, especially ones that use alliteration. Here are some similes that Roald Dahl uses to describe someone as slightly dotty:

as **batty** as a **bullfrog**

as **crazy** as a **crumpet**

as **dotty** as a **doughnut**

as **potty** as a **pilchard**

as **quacky** as a **duckhound**

as **dotty** as a **dogswoggler**

You can use the same techniques to make up your own dotty, silly similes. For an **extra-redunculous** simile, choose something that is spotted or dotty already for your comparison:

as **dotty** as a **currant bun**

as **dotty** as a **Dalmatian**

as **dotty** as a **Pink-Spotted Scrunch**

as **dotty** as a **Spotted Whangdoodle**

Not all similes have to be dotty however! You can turn any **extra-usual** creature into a silly simile.

as **crazy** as a **cockatootloo**

as **fussy** as a **fogglefrump**

as **grubby** as a **grobblesquirt**

as **quacky** as a **quogwinkle**

cockatootloo *noun* and fogglefrump *noun*

The *cockatootloo* and the *fogglefrump* are quiet and docile animals that live in Giant Country.

grobblesquirt *noun*

The *grobblesquirt* is a creature that is hunted by witches to make Formula 86 Delayed Action Mouse-Maker.

Quogwinkle *noun*

A *quogwinkle* is a creature from outer space that makes regular visits to Giant Country.

!!ROTSOME TIP!!
You can make silly similes with REDUNCULOUS objects, too:
as *silly* as a *sizzlepan*
as *daft* as a *doormat*

Explosive expletives

An *expletive* (say eks-**plee**-tiv) is a word you say when you are Very Cross Indeed about something. You may have heard grown-ups using expletives when they stub their toe or spill **frobscottle** on the carpet.

Here are some expletives that Roald Dahl invented, which will NOT get you into trouble with grown-ups, because they won't have heard of them before. (In fact, they might start using them, too.)

Gunghummers and bogswinkles!

A shower of glass fell upon the poor BFG. 'Gunghummers and bogswinkles!' he cried. 'What was that?'—THE BFG

The BFG also says:

Oh mince my maggots!
and
Oh swipe my swoggles!

But no one knows
exactly what his
swoggles are, or
how to swipe
them—which is
probably just as
well.

Great whistling whangdoodles!

This is one of Willy Wonka's favourite expletives. As **redunculous** things are always happening to Mr Wonka, he invents explosive expletives (as well as exploding sweets), so that he always has something to shout.

A *whangdoodle* is a terrifying creature that eats Oompa-Loompas. It is NOT the same as a *wangdoodle*, which is a *delumptious* sweet. (But if you give a *whangdoodle* a *wangdoodle*, it might stop eating Oompa-Loompas for a while.)

'Great whistling whangdoodles!' cried Mr Wonka, leaping so high in the air that when he landed his legs gave way and he crashed on to his backside.
—CHARLIE AND THE GREAT GLASS ELEVATOR

Snorting snozzwangers!

This is another favourite expression of Willy Wonka.
A *snozzwanger* is a deadly three-footed creature that
lives in Loompaland and preys on Oompa-Loompas.

*'Snorting snozzwangers!' he yelled, picking
himself up and waving the letter about as
though he were swatting mosquitoes.
'Listen to this, all of you!'*
—CHARLIE AND THE GREAT GLASS ELEVATOR

Whangdoodles!

!!ROTSOME TIP!!
You can use any word
that grown-ups do nOt
understand as an expletive
or other rude word.
For example, try saying:
Oh, FOGGLEFRUMPS!

or
*What a load of
BUNGSWOGGLE!*

A LOAD of... Poppyrot

All these words mean 'silly nonsense or rubbish'. They are very useful if someone (usually a grown-up) has said something that does not make sense—such as absolutely everything that Matilda's parents say.

balderdash *noun* (say **bol**-der-dash)
'Ridiculous!' they shouted. 'Absurd!'
'Poppycock!' 'Balderdash!' 'Madness!'
—JAMES AND THE GIANT PEACH

bunkum *noun*
'It's tying us up like a parcel!' yelled Grandma
Josephine. 'Bunkum!' said Mr Wonka.
—CHARLIE AND THE GREAT GLASS ELEVATOR

piffle *noun*
'Cut the piffle, Shanks,' snapped the President.
'This is a national emergency!'

—CHARLIE AND THE GREAT GLASS ELEVATOR

poppycock *noun*
You', said Mr Fox, 'are going to be poisoned.'
'Poppycock!' said Rat.
—FANTASTIC MR FOX

twaddle *noun* (rhymes with *waddle*)
School teachers suffer a good deal from
having to listen to this sort of twaddle
from proud parents.—MATILDA

Keep talking TWADDLE

Human beans say and think SO MANY silly things that there are never enough words to describe them all. In fact, there are as many words for 'nonsense' as there are *phizz-whizzing* sweets in Willy Wonka's factory!

Here are some more rude words that human beans and giants use to tell each other they are talking **twaddle**.

PIGSPIFFLE   **BUGSWALLOP**   **CRODSWOGGLE**

PIGWASH   **TUMMYROT**   **ROMMYTOT**

RUBBSQUASH   **SLUSHBUNGLE**   **POPPYROT**

The Air Marshal's face turned the colour of a ripe plum. He was not used to being told he was talking slushbungle.
—THE BFG

You can also say:

Your brain is full of bugwhiffles!

'If you will listen carefully I will try to explain,' said the BFG. *'But your brain is so full of bugwhiffles, I doubt you will ever understand.* —THE BFG

Roald Dahl made up lots of funny spoonerisms and malapropisms, like **catasterous disastrophe** and **skin and groans**. It is easy to make up your own, too, for example *belly jeans* from *jelly beans*.

What a load of bugswallop!

That's utter rubbsquash!

AND FINALLY...

Not ALL grown-ups are beastly, and not ALL human beans and creatures are *horrigust*. In fact, some are positively **buckswashling**. For every ghastly Miss Trunchbull there is a *gloriumptious* Miss Honey and for every **foulsome** Farmer Bean there is a Fantastic Mr Fox.

Roald Dahl invented lots of **not-so-rotsome** words, too, to describe *jumbly* giants, *delumptious* sweets, and other *phizz-whizzing* things.

You can find them ALL in the **fantabulous** *Oxford Roald Dahl Dictionary* . . . and of course in the splendiferous stories and poems of ROALD DAHL.